Weight Watchers™

CAREFREE
Christmas

LESLEY WATERS

SIMON & SCHUSTER
A VIACOM COMPANY

First published in Great Britain by Simon & Schuster, 1996
A Viacom Company

Copyright ©1996, Weight Watchers (UK) Ltd

Simon & Schuster Ltd
West Garden Place
Kendal Street
London W2 2AQ

First published 1996

Design: Green Moore Lowenhoff
Typesetting: Stylize
Photography: Karl Adamson
Styling: Maria Kelly
Food preparation: Jane Stevenson

Weight Watchers Publications Manager: Juliet Hudson
Weight Watchers Publications Assistant: Celia Whiston

ISBN 0-68481-802-7

Printed and bound in the United Kingdom by Print Wright Limited, Ipswich

Pictured on the front cover: Instant Spiced Christmas Pudding (page 38)

Recipe notes:
Egg size is medium (size 3), unless otherwise stated.
Vegetables are medium-size, unless otherwise stated.
The Points and Calorie values are for the main recipes only; remember to add
extra Points or Calories for the accompaniments.
1 tablespoon = 15 ml; 1 teaspoon = 5 ml.
Dried herbs can be substituted for fresh ones, but the flavour may not always
be as good. Halve the fresh herb quantity stated in the recipe.

Vegetarian recipes:
Ⓥ shows the recipe is vegetarian

Contents

Have yourself a Carefree Christmas

Food is everywhere this festive season, whether you are buying it, preparing it, or eating it – and this can make it a tense time for those of us wanting to shed a few pounds. When other people are indulging in lots of good things, we don't want to spoil the party atmosphere and, above all, we don't want to feel deprived.

Well don't worry, with Weight Watchers new Programme, 1,2,3 Success™, deprivation is most definitely a thing of the past. Nothing is forbidden, and all the delicious Christmas dishes that help create that festive feeling can be slotted into the Programme. You'll find them all here – roast turkey with an apple and thyme stuffing, a variation on mince pies that contains less fat than usual and a best-ever Christmas pud.

As well as recipes there's advice on how to have a calmer, more relaxing Christmas and tips to help you avoid any last-minute panic. And if that's not enough, we've included some nifty ideas for table decorations and gift wrappings. The *Carefree Christmas* cookbook will get you back in the festive spirit, and help you to create simple, scrumptious dishes that everyone can enjoy.

Conquering the Christmas Panic

Being one step ahead over the holiday period will put a stop to any feelings of panic as Christmas approaches. It really does pay off to plan your food preparation and to have a few extra ideas tucked up your sleeve for when unexpected guests appear. Every little bit of preparation that can be done in advance will help to make your Christmas more enjoyable.

Checklist – November

1. Make Christmas cake (see page 7).
2. Check all those kitchen appliances and tools that you don't normally use but will probably call into service over the Christmas period. Check cords and plugs and have some spare fuses just in case. Make sure that your knives are sharp for all that chopping and carving to be done. Check that you have big enough roasting and baking tins, enough large saucepans, and plenty of plates, cutlery and serving dishes.
3. If you are going to cook and freeze ahead, check that there is enough space in the freezer. It might be a good idea to defrost it and start afresh.

Two Weeks before Christmas

1. Do a storecupboard checklist. It's a good time to add some basic (and not so basic!) dried and canned goodies to your stores, for any unexpected guests or impromptu meals.
2. Decorate your Christmas cake (see pages 8 and 10).
3. Shop for all non-perishable and frozen items and sundries such as rubbish sacks, kitchen foil, clingfilm, kitchen paper, washing-up liquid etc.
4. Make a start on your table decorations for the Big Day – there are plenty of ideas throughout this book.

The Lead-up to the Main Event

1. A few days before Christmas, shop for dairy, poultry and meat products. Before buying the turkey consider the size of your oven – and don't buy one that won't fit inside!

Final shop is for fish, fruit, vegetables and fresh herbs. Remember that you can freeze leftover herbs for use another time.

2. If your turkey is frozen, calculate two or three days before Christmas how long it will need to thaw.

3. Also, two or three days before Christmas make the stuffing and Cranberry Relish (see pages 14 and 18) and, if you wish, a good stock for your gravy. Make your de-luxe mince pies etc.

Christmas Eve

1. Peel the potatoes, and cover them with cold salted water.
2. Wash and prepare your vegetables, and store in plastic bags in the refrigerator.
3. Clear kitchen worktops of anything that won't be needed, to give you extra space for the big event.
4. Have a relaxing bath and get a great night's sleep.

Danger! Christmas treats at large!

Picture how it'll be when you drop by at your Mum's, go to the office party, or spend an evening at a friend's house. Pretty much anywhere you go at this time of year you're going to find food. But forewarned is fore-armed!

Over the page you'll find a list of the treats and goodies that you're going to encounter most frequently along with their Points score and Calories.

However, if all this looks a little alarming, take heart! You don't have to spend so many of your precious Points and Calories on booze, nor do you have to miss out on any of the fun; here are some ideas for drinks that are more refreshing than the average party drink.

Tall, cool drinks

Dry white wine lasts much longer if you make it into a spritzer. Put it in a tall glass and top up with soda or sparking mineral water. Decorate with a slice of lemon or lime and plenty of ice. If you use half a small glass of wine you'll use up only $1/2$ Point.

A rosy spritzer can be made by pouring a small glass of rosé wine into a tall glass filled with crushed ice, and topping it up with low-Calorie tonic water. Finish with a slice of cucumber. Count this drink as 1 Point.

A cool glass of sangria can be made in a flash by pouring a small glass of red wine over a large glass of ice. Add a slice each of orange and lemon, and top with soda or low-Calorie lemonade. This drink is worth 1 Point.

Try a delicious non-alcoholic citrus cup drink. Simply pour a mixture of grapefruit, orange and lemon juice over a large glass of ice. Top with some chopped mint, a squeeze of lime, and fill to the brim with low-Calorie lemonade. Exotic fruit juice can be used in place of the citrus juices. Use a small glass of juice (100 ml) for $1/2$ Point.

Orange and apple juice poured over crushed ice with a pinch of cinnamon and then topped up with low-Calorie ginger beer makes quite a taste sensation. A small glass of juice (100 ml) is worth $1/2$ Point.

Nibbles and sweets	Points	Calories
100 g ($3^1/_2$ oz) dry roasted peanuts	$10^1/_2$	470
1 square of chocolate	1	150
1 After Eight mint	$^1/_2$	35
5 Matchmakers	$2^1/_2$	140
1 mince pie	4	250
1 (100 g/4 oz) slice of Christmas Cake	6	305
10 olives	$^1/_2$	30
60 g (2 oz) tortilla chips	4	245
30 g (1 oz) crisps	$2^1/_2$	155
30 g (1 oz) low-fat crisps	2	135
1 brazil nut	$^1/_2$	20
2 tablespoons bought tomato and chilli salsa	$^1/_2$	40
2 medium-sized satsumas	$^1/_2$	40
1 dried date	$^1/_2$	15
1 medium-sized fig	$^1/_2$	30
1 sausage roll	5	355

Drinks	Points	Calories
a gin and tonic	$1^1/_2$	80
a gin and diet tonic	1	50
a small glass of white wine (100 ml)	1	95
a small glass of sparkling white wine (100 ml)	1	120
a small glass of low-alcohol wine (100 ml)	$^1/_2$	35
a pub measure of dry Vermouth (48 ml)	$^1/_2$	70
a pint of lager	2	170
a pint of bitter	3	200
a pint of light ale	3	150
a can of cola	2	130
a can of diet cola	0	0
a small glass of fruit juice (100 ml)	$^1/_2$	70
soda water	0	0

First Things First

Make your Christmas a real cracker by being one step ahead. There are so many things that need to be done over this festive time – a little bit of planning and preparation can help you fit it all in and, most importantly, leave you enough time to enjoy yourself with family and friends. The easy-bake Christmas cake in this chapter can be prepared up to two months ahead of time, and I've also included some simple, but stylish cake decorations that take no time at all.

When preparing party nibbles, sausage rolls are a bit predictable – as well as full of Points! So why not try some of the ideas in this chapter? – they're easy to put together, healthier than conventional nibbles, low in Points and totally scrumptious!

Tutti-Frutti Christmas Cake

Allow to cool before wrapping in greaseproof paper. Wrap again in kitchen foil and then store in an airtight container for up to two months.

Makes: 18 cm (7-inch) cake (18 slices)
Preparation time: 20 minutes + 2–2¹/₂ hours baking
Freezing: not recommended
Points per slice: 1¹/₂
Total Points per recipe: 27
Calories per slice: 175

Ⓥ if using free-range eggs

1 teaspoon sunflower oil for greasing
120 g (4 oz) black treacle

120 g (4 oz) margarine
3 eggs, beaten
150 g (5 oz) plain flour
a pinch of salt
1 teaspoon mixed spice
120 g (4 oz) sultanas
120 g (4 oz) raisins
120 g (4 oz) currants
120 g (4 oz) glacé cherries, halved and rinsed
2 tablespoons medium-dry sherry
grated zest and juice of 1 orange

❶ Grease the base and sides of an 18 cm (7-inch) cake tin with the sunflower oil, and line with greaseproof paper or baking parchment.
❷ Preheat the oven to Gas Mark 2/150°C/300°F.
❸ In a large mixing bowl beat together the treacle and margarine. Gradually beat the eggs into this mixture and sift in the flour, salt and mixed spice. Add the dry fruits, cherries, sherry, and orange zest and juice. Fold in gently.
❹ Turn the mixture into the prepared tin and level the surface, making a slight dip in the centre. Bake in the oven for 2–2¹/₂ hours. If the cake begins to look too brown, cover the top with a piece of greaseproof paper.
❺ Test the cake with a skewer; if it comes out clean, the cake is cooked. If not, then give it a little longer in the oven. Allow the cake to cool in the tin for 15 minutes, then turn it out on to a wire rack. When completely cool remove the greaseproof paper or baking parchment. Wrap in foil or clean greaseproof paper and store in an airtight tin.

For a special meal, tie napkins in some pretty gold braid. What could be simpler or more festive? If you're running out of plates or you have an unusual-shaped cake, cover an old wooden bread board with gold paint.

Grilled Marzipan Cake

Makes: enough to cover a 18 cm (7-inch) cake
    (18 slices)
Preparation time: 30 minutes
Freezing: not recommended
Points per serving: 3
Total Points per recipe: 54
Calories per serving: 60

2 teaspoons runny honey
2 teaspoons icing sugar
240 g (8 oz) marzipan
1 small egg, beaten

Ⓥ if using a free-range egg

❶ Brush the top of the cake with the honey. Set aside.
❷ Preheat the grill.
❸ Dust the work surface with the icing sugar and roll out half the marzipan to fit on the top of the cake.
❹ Roll out the remaining marzipan and cut into generous holly leaves and small berries.
❺ Brush the top of the cake lightly with beaten egg. Lay the holly leaves and berries over the top in an attractive fashion. Brush lightly again with the beaten egg.
❻ Put the cake on a baking sheet and set under the grill until it turns golden brown – watch closely as this will happen very quickly!
❼ Tie a ribbon round your cake and decorate with a sprig of real holly.

Christmas may be a holiday, but if you're the one who does the shopping, decides what to cook and cooks it, ferries the kids about, etc., it can be a pretty stressful time. When lying down in bed or in the bath, try relaxing all your muscles one at a time, starting from your toes and slowly working up your body. Close your eyes, breathe deeply and try to clear your mind and relax.

Higgledy-Piggledy Glazed Fruit Cake
Grilled Marzipan Cake

Higgledy-Piggledy Glazed Fruit Cake

This is a really simple, but festive idea for decorating your cake without piling on too many Points and without giving yourself the hassle of icing. For a really classy effect use the natural-colour glacé cherries that are now available.

Makes: enough to cover an 18 cm (7-inch) cake
(18 slices)
Preparation time: 30 minutes
Freezing: not recommended
Points per serving: 1
Total Points per recipe: 18
Calories per serving: 75

3 tablespoons reduced-sugar apricot jam
120 g (4 oz) ready-to-eat dried apricots
60 g (2 oz) glacé cherries, rinsed and dried
1 small jar of stem ginger, rinsed, dried, and
  sliced thickly
90 g (3 oz) walnut halves

1 Wrap a cake frill or a pretty ribbon around your cake. The frill or ribbon should be slightly higher than the cake. Secure with a pin or glue.

2 In a small saucepan heat the jam. Push it through a fine sieve and set aside.

3 In a mixing bowl, toss together the apricots, cherries, ginger and walnuts. Pour in the warm apricot glaze and toss again. Pile the glazed fruit on top of your cake in a higgledy-piggledy fashion. Alternatively, brush the top of the cake with a little apricot glaze and arrange the fruit, ginger and walnuts in diagonal rows or patterns on top of the cake. Lightly brush again with apricot glaze (thinned-down with a little water if it goes too thick).

Try to set aside one day when you can concentrate on preparing most of your Christmas food. Being well organised means less hassle and makes for a truly carefree Christmas.

Pear and Cheese Parcels

These delicious warm pear and cheese parcels are a great party idea that could easily double as a light lunch if served with a crisp salad. Do try filo pastry if you haven't already done so. It's low in fat and needs no rolling. Choose a half-fat cheese to keep down the Calories, but do make sure it's a cheese with plenty of flavour, like a mature Cheddar or perhaps a Stilton.

Makes: 18
Preparation and cooking time: 35 minutes
Freezing: recommended
Points per parcel: 1
Total Points per recipe: 18
Calories per parcel: 40

V if using a free-range egg and vegetarian Cheddar

1 teaspoon olive oil
half a bunch of spring onions, chopped
2 large ripe pears, peeled, cored and diced
120 g (4 oz) well-flavoured half-fat Cheddar, grated
1 egg
180 g (6 oz) filo pastry
1 tablespoon poppy seeds
salt and freshly ground black pepper

1 In a small saucepan heat the olive oil and fry the spring onions until softened.

2 Add the diced pears and toss over a fierce heat for a further 2 minutes. Remove the pan from the heat and set aside to cool.

3 Preheat the oven to Gas Mark 6/200°C/400°F.

4 Add the grated Cheddar to the onion and pear mixture and season to taste.

5 In a small bowl beat the egg with a pinch of salt and 2 tablespoons of cold water to make a light egg wash.

6 Cut each sheet of filo pastry into 5 cm (2-inch) strips.

7 Brush a very light covering of egg wash over each strip of filo pastry.

8 Place a spoonful of filling at one end of each strip.

9 Fold the corner of the pastry over the filling to form a triangle. Fold the pastry strip over and over, keeping the triangle shape and making sure all the filling is enclosed, until you reach the end. Repeat with the other strips and the remaining filling.

10 Brush the parcels with the egg wash and sprinkle with poppy seeds. Place on a lightly greased non-stick baking sheet and bake for 12 minutes or until golden brown. Serve warm.

Hot Spicy Prawn Salsa

Serve this fiery fiesta of flavours with a selection of low-Calorie crackers or melba toast. Remember to add the Points.

Serves: 6
Preparation time: 10 minutes + 30 minutes
   marinating
Freezing: not recommended
Points per serving: 1
Total Points per recipe: 6
Calories per serving: 50

2 large tomatoes, chopped
1 onion, chopped

1 red pepper, chopped
a handful of fresh coriander
grated zest and juice of 1 lime
420 g (14 oz) canned chopped tomatoes, drained
1 teaspoon sugar
1 tablespoon white wine vinegar
Tabasco sauce, to taste
120 g (4 oz) cooked peeled prawns
salt and freshly ground black pepper

1 In a food processor blend together the fresh tomatoes, onion, red pepper, coriander, lime zest and juice for 30 seconds. Turn this mixture into a bowl and add all of the remaining ingredients except for the prawns. Season to taste and leave to marinate for 30 minutes.

2 Add the prawns just before serving.
3 Pile the salsa into a shallow serving dish, place on a platter or flat basket and surround with crackers and melba toast.

Orangey Chick Pea Dip

This is a scrumptious, but lighter, version of hummus which will certainly tickle those taste buds. Serve with warm pitta bread, rye crackers or vegetable crudités. Remember to add the correct number of Points.

Serves: 4
Preparation time: 10 minutes
Freezing: not recommended
Points per serving: 1¹/₂
Total Points per recipe: 6
Calories per serving: 120

(V)

420 g (14 oz) canned chick peas, drained
2 tablespoons low-fat fromage frais
2 garlic cloves, crushed
juice of 1 lemon
1 large orange, peeled and segmented
2 teaspoons olive oil
2 tablespoons roughly chopped flat-leaf parsley
   or coriander
salt and freshly ground black pepper

1 Put three-quarters of the chick peas in a food processor with the fromage frais, garlic and lemon juice. Whizz until smooth and creamy, adding a little water if necessary.
2 Toss the remaining chick peas in a small bowl with the orange segments, olive oil and parsley or coriander. Season to taste.

3 Pile the creamy dip into a shallow serving dish and scatter over the orange, chick pea and parsley garnish. Grind plenty of black pepper over the top. Chill until required.

Hot Spicy Prawn Salsa
Pear and Cheese Parcels

Meals in the Main

Most of us like to cook at least one meal for family and friends over the holiday period. It needn't be a stressful or daunting experience. Have a look through the recipes in this chapter – they're all simple to prepare and are guaranteed to give you and your guests maximum taste, while still allowing you to stick to your diet.

Traditional Roast Turkey with Thyme and Apple Stuffing

Cook the turkey breast-side down to keep the meat juicy and tender.

Serves: 6–12 (with plenty of leftovers)
Preparation time: 15 minutes + 4 hours cooking + resting
Freezing: not recommended
Points per serving of turkey (3 slices): 2
Points per serving of stuffing: 1½
Total Points for stuffing: 18
Calories per serving of turkey (3 slices): 115
Calories per serving of stuffing: 60

6.5 kg (14 lb) oven-ready turkey
2 pears, cored and quartered
2 apples, cored and quartered
1 onion, peeled and quartered
4 bay leaves
For the stuffing:
1 onion, chopped finely
3 lean bacon rashers, chopped
2 celery sticks, chopped finely
2 dessert apples, cored and chopped
1 tablespoon chopped fresh thyme
240 g (8 oz) fresh white breadcrumbs
2 eggs, beaten
salt and freshly ground black pepper

1 Preheat the oven to Gas Mark 7/220°C/425°F.

2 First make the stuffing. In a saucepan fry the onion, bacon and celery for 1 minute. Add the apples and thyme, cover and cook gently for a further 4 minutes.

3 In a mixing bowl combine this mixture with the breadcrumbs and beaten eggs. Season to taste.

4 Put the pears, apples, onion and bay leaves in the turkey's cavity.

5 Pack the stuffing loosely into the neck of the turkey and tuck the neck skin flap under the turkey and secure with a skewer. Put any remaining stuffing in a small ovenproof dish and set it to one side.

6 Put the turkey on a rack over a large roasting pan, breast-side down, so that the cooking juices keep the breast meat moist and tender. Cover loosely with foil and cook for 40 minutes.

7 Reduce the oven temperature to Gas Mark 4/180°C/350°F and cook the turkey for 1 hour. Remove the turkey from the oven and very carefully turn it over. Replace the foil and cook for a further 2 hours, basting occasionally.

8 Remove the foil and baste the turkey. Cook the turkey without the foil for 20–30 minutes more to brown it. To check that it is cooked, pierce the thigh with a skewer and if the juices run clear the bird is cooked, but if there is still a trace of pink then it will need extra time in the oven.

9 When the turkey is cooked, allow it to rest for 30 minutes before carving.

Traditional Roast Turkey with Thyme and Apple Stuffing

Onion and Thyme Gravy

Traditional turkey gravy is made with the stock from the turkey giblets. Here's a quick tasty variation using vegetable stock.

Serves: 6
Preparation and cooking time: 30 minutes
Freezing: recommended for up to 2 months
Points per serving: $^{1}/_{2}$
Total Points per recipe: 3
Calories per serving: 60

Ⓥ

2 teaspoons sunflower oil
2 onions, chopped very finely
1 large flat mushroom, peeled and chopped
very finely
1 tablespoon chopped fresh thyme
2 teaspoons flour
750 ml (1¼ pints) vegetable stock
150 ml (¼ pint) red wine or white wine
1 bay leaf
¹/₂ teaspoon gravy browning (optional)
salt and freshly ground black pepper

❶ In a saucepan heat the oil and gently cook the onions for 1 minute. Cover with a lid, reduce the heat and cook for a further 4 minutes or until the onions have softened. Remove the lid, and increase the heat under the saucepan. Fry until the onion is well coloured.

❷ Add the chopped mushroom and thyme to the saucepan and fry for 1 minute. Add the flour and

cook for a further minute. Gradually pour in the stock and wine, stirring constantly. Add the bay leaf and gravy browning (if needed), bring to the boil and season with salt and pepper. Simmer gently for 20 minutes.

Cook's note: save any water you use to cook vegetables as this makes a good stock.

For impressive, but simple, gift and table decorations buy special curling ribbon. You make the curls by pulling the ribbon tautly over the blade of a pair of scissors.
If you have a lovely old decanter or other piece of glass or china that you bring out at Christmas, try draping a piece of gold cord with a tassel around it – very easy, very festive.

Rustic Roast Potatoes

Serves: 6
Preparation time: 1½ hours
Freezing: not recommended
Points per serving: 2½
Total Points per recipe: 15
Calories per serving: 150

(V)

2 tablespoons sunflower oil
2 tablespoons light soy sauce
1 teaspoon honey
2 garlic cloves, crushed
freshly ground black pepper
1.05 kg (2¼ lb) potatoes, scrubbed well

❶ Preheat the oven to Gas Mark 5/190°C/375°F.
❷ In a large mixing bowl, stir together the oil, soy sauce, honey, garlic and black pepper.
❸ Cut the potatoes in half lengthways and, with a small knife, cut lightly into the potato to score a lattice pattern.

❹ Place the potatoes into the oil and soy sauce mixture and toss well to coat them thoroughly.
❺ Place on a shallow non-stick baking tray and cook for 1¼ hours until crisp and golden brown.

Christmas Baked Ham with a Marmalade Glaze

Serves: 8–12 with leftovers
Preparation time: soaking overnight + 10 minutes
   + 2 hours cooking + 20 minutes cooling
Freezing: not recommended
Points per 90 g (3 oz) serving: 2½
Total Points per recipe: 56
Calories per 90 g (3 oz) serving: 200

1.75 kg (4 lb) joint of prime gammon
1 onion
1 carrot, scrubbed
2 bay leaves
12 peppercorns
whole cloves
3 tablespoons sharp marmalade

❶ Soak the gammon in cold water overnight.
❷ Place the gammon in a large saucepan and cover with fresh cold water. Add the vegetables, bay leaves and peppercorns. Bring to the boil slowly, cover with a lid and simmer very gently for 1½ hours.
❸ Preheat the oven to Gas Mark 7/220°C/424°F. Allow the joint of gammon to cool in the cooking liquid for 20 minutes. Remove from the cooking liquid and, using a sharp knife, carefully remove the skin and most of the underlying fat, leaving only a thin layer of fat.
❹ Cut a lattice pattern over the gammon. Press a clove into each diamond segment. Smear over the marmalade. Bake the joint for about 20 minutes or until golden brown and lightly caramelised.
❺ Serve hot or cold with the Cranberry Relish (page 18).

Cranberry Relish

This relish is whizzed together from absolutely fresh ingredients. Because it's fresh it needs far less sugar than a shop-bought relish or pickle would contain – and because it's fresh it's really healthy and packed with flavour.

Serves: 12
Preparation time: 10 minutes
Freezing: not recommended
Points per serving: ¹/₂
Total Points per recipe: 6
Calories per serving: 20

(V)

1 medium-sized orange, washed
480 g (1 lb) cranberries, thawed if frozen
1–2 tablespoons icing sugar

❶ Roughly chop the whole unpeeled orange. Blend it in a food processor until almost a pulp. Add the cranberries and sugar and continue to blend until the cranberries are finely chopped.

❷ Spoon the cranberry relish into a serving dish. Cover and refrigerate until required. It will keep for several days in the refrigerator.

Beef and Chestnut Stew

This stew is even better if made a day before you want to eat it; this allows flavours to develop even more. If you don't want to use beef you can try this dish with lean diced leg of lamb.

Serves: 6
Preparation and cooking time: 3¹/₂ hours
Freezing: not recommended
Points per serving: 7¹/₂
Total Points per recipe: 45
Calories per serving: 290

2 large onions, sliced
2 teaspoons sunflower oil

1 garlic clove, crushed
720 g (1¹/₂ lb) lean diced braising steak
1 tablespoon flour
150 ml (¹/₄ pint) red wine
900 ml (1¹/₂ pints) beef stock
180 g (6 oz) peeled chestnuts
180 g (6 oz) pitted prunes, halved
1 bay leaf
salt and freshly ground black pepper

❶ Preheat the oven to Gas Mark 2/150°C/300°F.
❷ In a large frying-pan gently fry the onions in the sunflower oil until softened and browned. Add the garlic and cook for 1 minute. Transfer the onions to a plate and set aside.
❸ Place the frying-pan back on the stove over a fierce heat and quickly brown the beef. Add the onions to the beef and sprinkle over the flour.

Cook, stirring, for a further 30 seconds. Pour in the wine and stock and stir until boiling. Add the remaining ingredients and season well. Transfer the beef into a casserole dish, cover with a lid and cook in the oven for 2¹/₂–3 hours or until the meat is very tender. Remove the bay leaf before serving. Serve with Parsnip and Potato Mash (page 22).

Beef and Chestnut Stew
Christmas Baked Ham with a Marmalade Glaze
Cranberry Relish

Aubergine Parcels with Red Pepper Sauce

Serves: 6
Preparation and cooking time: 40 minutes
Freezing: not recommended
Points per serving: 5
Total Points per recipe: 30
Calories per serving: 200

Ⓥ

2 teaspoons sunflower oil
1 onion, chopped
1 large aubergine, diced

2 dessert apples, peeled, cored and chopped
1 garlic clove, crushed
a bunch of fresh basil, chopped
6 sheets of filo pastry (25 cm × 23 cm/
    10 inches × 9 inches), thawed if frozen
2 tablespoons olive oil
salt and freshly ground black pepper
For the red pepper sauce:
2 red peppers, halved, de-seeded and sliced
1 teaspoon sunflower oil
$^1/_2$ teaspoon chilli powder
480 g (1 lb) creamed tomatoes

❶ In a saucepan heat the sunflower oil and fry the onion, aubergine and apples gently until softened. Stir in the garlic and chopped basil. Season to taste and set to one side to cool.

❷ In a saucepan fry the red peppers in the sunflower oil for 1 minute. Add the chilli powder and cook for a further 30 seconds. Pour in the creamed tomatoes, bring to the boil and simmer for 15–20 minutes, adding a little water if the sauce becomes too thick. Season to taste with salt and pepper.

❸ Preheat the oven to Gas Mark 6/200°C/400°F. Cut the filo pastry sheets in half. Take two pieces and brush each lightly with the olive oil (keep the remaining filo covered with a damp tea towel so it doesn't dry out).

❹ Sandwich the two layers together. Spoon a layer of aubergine mixture on to the filo square allowing a 2.5 cm (1-inch) border all the way around. Roll into a sausage and gently shape into a crescent. Place the crescent on a non-stick baking sheet. Repeat this process with the remaining filo and filling until you have made six mini crescents.

❺ Brush the crescents lightly with the remaining olive oil and bake for 15 minutes or until golden brown and crisp. Serve with the pepper sauce and Creamy Minty Peas (page 29).

Creamy Minty Peas
Aubergine Parcels with Red Pepper Sauce

Sausage and Cranberry Stew

Serves: 4
Preparation and cooking time: 30 minutes
Freezing: not recommended
Points per serving: 3
Total Points per recipe: 12
Calories per serving: 235

2 teaspoons sunflower oil
3 leeks, washed and sliced finely
8 low-fat sausages, twisted and cut into two
450 ml (³/₄ pint) vegetable stock
a sprig of fresh rosemary
240 g (8 oz) fresh or frozen cranberries
1 teaspoon sugar
2 teaspoons Dijon mustard
salt and freshly ground black pepper
1 teaspoon chopped fresh parsley, to garnish

❶ In a large frying-pan heat the oil and cook the leeks for 1 minute. Cover and continue to cook gently until soft and golden brown.

❷ Add the sausages and fry until lightly browned and almost cooked.

❸ Add the stock, rosemary, cranberries and sugar.

Cover and simmer gently for 10–12 minutes.

❹ Stir the mustard into the sausages and season to taste. Scatter over the parsley and serve with vegetables and Parsnip and Potato Mash.

Parsnip and Potato Mash

Serves: 6
Preparation and cooking time: 40 minutes
Freezing: not recommended
Points per serving: 2¹/₂
Total Points per recipe: 15
Calories per serving: 150

480 g (1 lb) potatoes, peeled and cut in
    even-sized pieces
960 g (2 lb) parsnips, peeled and cut in
    5 cm (2-inch) pieces
2 tablespoons low-fat fromage frais
2 tablespoons chopped fresh parsley, to garnish
salt and freshly ground black pepper

❶ In a large saucepan boil the potatoes until half cooked. Add the parsnips and continue cooking until both are tender.

❷ Drain well, return to the saucepan and mash thoroughly (or briefly whizz in a food processor). Stir in the fromage frais, parsley and seasoning to taste.

Decorate table napkins with a tiny present – something Christmassy but very cheap and cheerful. We used a Father Christmas pencil (see opposite) and tied it to the napkin with a ribbon that matched the other table accessories.

Stir-fried Savoy Cabbage with Pear
Parsnip and Potato Mash
Sausage and Cranberry Stew

Fish Florentine

Serves: 6

Preparation time: 45 minutes + 45 minutes cooking

Freezing: recommended

Points per serving: 5

Total Points per recipe: 30

Calories per serving: 335

480 g (1 lb) white fish fillets
480 g (1 lb) smoked fish fillets
1 bay leaf
420 g (14 oz) canned chopped tomatoes
1 carton creamed tomatoes

1 large red pepper, halved, cored and sliced
6 cardamom pods, crushed (optional)
360 g (12 oz) frozen spinach, thawed
1 teaspoon ground nutmeg
salt and freshly ground black pepper

For the topping:

1.1 kg (2$\frac{1}{2}$ lb) potatoes, washed, scrubbed and cut in 1 cm ($\frac{1}{2}$-inch) cubes
1 tablespoon sunflower oil
a bunch of spring onions, chopped
2 teaspoons turmeric
2 tablespoons dried breadcrumbs

❶ Preheat the oven to Gas Mark 5/190°C/375°F. Place the fish and bay leaf in an ovenproof dish, skin-side up, and barely cover with water. Bake for about 15 minutes, until the skin peels easily. Allow to cool.

❷ In a saucepan, combine the canned and creamed tomatoes, sliced pepper, crushed cardamom pods (if using) and 4 tablespoons of the fish poaching liquid. Bring to the boil, cover and simmer for 20 minutes. Meanwhile, boil the potatoes until just tender, but so that they still keep their shape.

❸ Drain and squeeze any excess liquid from the thawed spinach. Season with salt, pepper and nutmeg. Spread a layer of spinach in a large, shallow ovenproof dish. Remove the skin from the fish. Gently flake the fish and scatter over the spinach. Spoon over the cooled tomato sauce.

❹ Heat the oil in a frying-pan and add the spring onions and turmeric and fry gently for 1 minute. Add the potatoes and gently toss. Spoon the seasoned potatoes evenly over the top of the tomato sauce. Scatter over the breadcrumbs and bake for 45–50 minutes or until golden brown.

For table decorations that are bound to catch your guests' eye, put a tiny pressie (it needn't be much – just a chocolate or two or a couple of bath oil beads) in a little box. Wrap in tissue paper and ribbon. Add a flower, real or artificial, or a little piece of ivy and slip inside a napkin.

Chinese-style Green Beans
Fish Florentine

Cheap pearl necklaces look very effective draped around gold candles. Add some pretty glass pebbles.

Citrus Cod

Serves: 6

Preparation and cooking time: 15 minutes +
    30 minutes marinating

Freezing: not recommended

Points per serving: 3

Total Points per recipe: 18

Calories per serving: 160

6 × 150 g (5 oz) cod steaks

For the marinade:

grated zest and juice of 1 lime

grated zest and juice of 1 lemon

grated zest and juice of 1 orange

2 tablespoons virgin olive oil

freshly ground black pepper

❶ In a large dish mix together the marinade ingredients. Turn the cod steaks in the marinade and leave to stand for 30 minutes.

❷ Preheat the grill. Place the cod steaks on a non-stick baking tray and brush over any remaining marinade. Grill under a medium heat for 4 minutes on each side or until just cooked. Serve with the Spiced Lentils and Leeks (page 30).

Work a little exercise into your day. Not only is this great for the body, but it can also reduce stress. So when you're doing any work in the house, get moving! Wear comfortable clothes and trainers, put on some lively music and dance through your chores. Better still, clear the floor for a boogie/dance workout.

*Citrus Cod
Spiced Lentils and Leeks*

Chinese-style Green Beans

Serves: 6
Preparation and cooking time: 15 minutes
Freezing: not recommended
Points per serving: ½
Total Points per recipe: 3
Calories per serving: 60

Ⓥ

720 g (1½ lb) french or dwarf beans, topped
  and tailed
1 teaspoon sunflower oil
5 cm (2-inch) piece of fresh root ginger, peeled
  and grated
1 garlic clove, crushed
3 tablespoons light soy sauce
juice of 1 orange
1 teaspoon sesame oil
freshly ground black pepper

❶ Place the beans in a saucepan of boiling water and cook until just tender.

❷ Meanwhile heat the sunflower oil in a small saucepan and gently fry the ginger and garlic for 30 seconds. Remove from the heat and stir in the soy sauce, orange juice and sesame oil.

❸ Drain the beans well and return to the saucepan. Pour over the ginger mixture, season with pepper, toss well and serve at once.

Cook's note: If you don't use all the fresh root ginger, keep it in the freezer for use later.

For a great night's sleep, drink plenty of water throughout the day and not too much alcohol or caffeine (that means tea as well as coffee). Make sure your bedroom is the right temperature and that your bed and pillows are comfortable. Have time to relax before going to bed – perhaps take a warm bath or shower, or even set out your clothes and make a list for the day ahead. Sleep gives your body a chance to restore itself, so you awake feeling refreshed and healed.

Creamy Minty Peas

This dish can be served as an accompanying vegetable or made into a delicious creamy pea soup. You could try minted peas if you can't get fresh mint – it's doubtful however that the flavour will be so good.

Serves: 6
Preparation and cooking time: 15 minutes
Freezing: recommended
Points per serving: 2
Total Points per recipe: 12
Calories per serving: 85

Ⓥ

720 g (1¹/₂ lb) frozen peas
1 onion, grated
a bunch of fresh mint
1 garlic clove, crushed
salt and freshly ground black pepper

❶ Place the peas and the onion in a saucepan. Pour over enough boiling water to barely cover and cook the peas for 5 minutes until tender. Remove the mint leaves from their stalks and set aside.
❷ Drain the peas, reserving the cooking liquid. Blend the peas, onion, garlic and mint leaves in a food processor with a little of the cooking liquid until creamy and smooth. Season to taste.

Cook's note: to make a delicious low-fat soup, add some more cooking liquid to the purée and blend until creamy and soup-like. Reheat the soup and season well. Ladle into warm soup bowls and scatter some cooked chopped gammon or turkey over the top. Remember to add the extra Points.

Green Peas cooked with Little Onions and Tomatoes

Canned cherry tomatoes are widely available. Look for them next to the ordinary canned tomatoes.

Serves: 6
Preparation and cooking time: 25 minutes
Freezing: not recommended
Points per serving: 1
Total Points per recipe: 6
Calories per serving: 95

Ⓥ

2 teaspoons olive oil
240 g (8 oz) button onions, peeled
480 g (1 lb) frozen garden peas
300 ml (¹/₂ pint) vegetable stock
a pinch of sugar
1 teaspoon dried oregano
420 g (14 oz) canned cherry tomatoes
salt and freshly ground black pepper
fresh chopped parsley, to garnish

❶ Heat the oil in a large saucepan and gently fry the button onions. Add the peas, stock, sugar and oregano and season well. Cover and cook for 6 minutes or until the peas are just cooked.

❷ Stir in the cherry tomatoes with their juices. Heat through and check the seasoning. Serve with a scattering of parsley.

Spiced Lentils and Leeks

A tasty partner to accompany any grilled fish (especially Citrus Cod on page 26)
or great served with cold cuts on Boxing Day.

Serves: 6
Preparation and cooking time: 35 minutes
Freezing: not recommended
Points per serving: 3
Total Points per recipe: 18
Calories per serving: 295

Ⓥ

2 teaspoons sunflower oil
480 g (1 lb) leeks, washed and sliced finely
3 garlic cloves, crushed
2 tablespoons medium-strength curry paste
1 bay leaf
480 g (1 lb) orange lentils, rinsed
about 1 litre (1³/₄ pints) vegetable stock
2 tablespoons low-fat natural yogurt
salt and freshly ground black pepper

❶ In a large saucepan heat the oil and fry the leeks until softened and slightly coloured.

❷ Stir in the garlic and curry paste and fry gently for 1 minute.

❸ Add the bay leaf, lentils and stock, and season well. Simmer for about 15–20 minutes or until the lentils are just tender (adding extra stock if necessary).

❹ Pile into a serving dish. Drizzle over the natural yogurt and grind over some black pepper.

Aromatic Carrot Purée

This recipe can be served as an accompanying vegetable or it can be transformed into a heart-warming tasty soup.

Serves: 6
Preparation and cooking time: 25 minutes
Freezing: recommended
Points per serving: 0
Total Points per recipe: 0
Calories per serving: 55

Ⓥ

1.25 kg (3 lb) carrots, peeled and sliced
a bunch of coriander
salt and freshly ground black pepper

❶ Place the carrots in a large saucepan and cover with water. Boil until tender. Remove the coriander leaves from their stalks and set aside.

❷ Drain the carrots, reserving the cooking juice. Blend the carrots in a food processor with the coriander leaves and a little of the cooking liquid until a creamy thick mixture is achieved. Season to taste with salt and freshly ground black pepper.

Cook's note: to make a delicious low-Point, low-Calorie soup, simply add extra cooking liquid when blending the carrots and blend until creamy and soup-like. Reheat, season and ladle into warm bowls. Trickle over a swirl of low-fat natural yogurt just before serving. Remember to add the extra Points.

Stir-fried Savoy Cabbage with Pear

Do try using the juniper berries if you haven't before. They add an extra-special flavour and aroma to this dish of stir-fried greens. If you should happen to wonder what the taste of juniper berries reminds you of – well, juniper is used to flavour gin.

Serves: 6
Preparation and cooking time: 20 minutes
Freezing: not recommended
Points per serving: 1
Total Points per recipe: 6
Calories per serving: 75

Ⓥ

2 teaspoons sunflower oil
2 onions, sliced
2 teaspoons sugar
1 tablespoon white wine vinegar
3 pears, cored and sliced
12 juniper berries, crushed (optional)
480 g (1 lb) savoy cabbage, shredded finely, washed and drained
$1/_2$ teaspoon ground nutmeg
salt and freshly ground black pepper

❶ Heat the oil in a large saucepan or wok and fry the onions gently until softened. Add the sugar and cook for a further 2–3 minutes until the onions start to caramelise (go golden brown).

❷ Add the wine vinegar, sliced pears, juniper berries (if using) and cabbage to the onions and toss well together. Season with nutmeg, salt and pepper.

❸ Increase the heat, cover with a lid and cook for 4–5 minutes, stirring occasionally until the cabbage is just cooked. Pile into a dish and serve immediately.

Sweet Nothings

t's important not to feel deprived at Christmas. These sweet sensations will be popular with all the family, and you can indulge in them safe in the knowledge that they form part of your diet. There are some wonderful treats here, including a lighter version of Christmas pudding that you can make on Christmas Eve, or even on the day itself if you wish.

Red Berry Jelly

Serves: 6
Preparation time: 15 minutes + 3 hours setting
Freezing: not recommended
Points per serving: 1½
Total Points per recipe: 9
Calories per serving: 100

1½ **sachets of powdered gelatine**
1 **tablespoon caster sugar**
750 ml (1¼ **pints) red grape juice**
480 g (1 lb) **frozen summer fruits, just thawed**
240 g (8 oz) **strawberries, washed**

Ⓥ if replacing gelatine with vegetarian substitute

❶ Put 4 tablespoons of water into a small saucepan and evenly sprinkle over the gelatine. Set aside for 5 minutes for the gelatine to 'sponge'.
❷ In another saucepan gently heat the sugar and grape juice together until the sugar dissolves.
❸ Dissolve the gelatine over a gentle heat and when clear stir it into the grape juice syrup.
❹ Place the fruit into a large oval or round 1.2-litre (2-pint) shallow dish, reserving a few strawberries for

garnish. Pour the grape juice over the fruits and refrigerate until set.
❺ You can either serve the jelly from the dish or dip the dish briefly in boiling water and turn out on to a platter. Decorate with the reserved strawberries.

Cook's note: if you wish you can make individual jellies in cups or ramekins – these will set far quicker.

Take a little flowerpot and paint the rim gold and the sides cream. Stencil on some leaf-shapes in gold. Stand a white candle in the pot and surround with florist's foam. Paint some nuts (still in shell) gold and glue on top of the florist's foam to cover. Add a bunch of cinnamon sticks tied with gold ribbon.

Ginger Syllabub
Red Berry Jelly

Passion Cream Dome with Exotic Fruits

You can use any attractive combination of fruits you like.

Serves: 6
Preparation and cooking time: 20 minutes
Freezing: not recommended
Points per serving: 5$^1/_2$
Total Points per recipe: 33
Calories per serving: 200

(V)

3 oranges
360 g (12 oz) low-fat cottage cheese, drained
150 ml ($^1/_4$ pint) reduced-fat whipping cream
3 teaspoons icing sugar
4 kiwis, peeled and sliced
2 bananas, sliced thickly on the diagonal, tossed
   in a little lemon juice
1 large ripe mango, peeled and cut into strips
3 ripe passion fruit, halved with pulp scooped out

1 Grate the zest from two of the oranges and set aside. Using a wooden spoon, push the cottage cheese through a sieve (this takes seconds) into a small bowl. Whip the cream until stiff peaks form.

2 In a mixing bowl gently fold the sieved cheese and the whipped cream together and stir in the icing sugar and orange zest.

3 Pile the flavoured cream mixture into the centre of a large platter and, using a small knife or spatula, shape into a dome. Chill well.

4 Meanwhile prepare the fruit. Using a sharp knife, peel and slice the oranges. Arrange all the fruit attractively around the cream dome. Spoon the passion fruit pulp over the top of the dome and serve.

Drunken Fruit Salad

A fruit salad with a real kick!

Serves: 6
Preparation time: 5 minutes
Freezing: not recommended
Points per serving: 1
Total Points per recipe: 6
Calories per serving: 90

(V)

a selection of prepared fresh fruits
   (e.g. strawberries, ripe plums,
   satsuma segments and peach slices)
juice of 2 oranges
1 tablespoon chopped fresh mint (optional)
300 ml ($^1/_2$ pint) chilled, sweet white wine
crushed ice, to serve

1 In a mixing bowl gently toss together the fruit with the orange juice and chopped mint (if using). Divide the fruit between six glasses and top each with some sweet white wine. Chill for 1 hour in the fridge.

2 To finish simply scatter with a little crushed ice and serve at once.

Passion Cream Dome with Exotic Fruits
Drunken Fruit Salad

Chocolate Meringue Roulade with Black Cherries

Serves: 6
Preparation time: 10 minutes + 20 minutes baking
Freezing: not recommended
Points per serving: 4$^1/_2$
Total Points per recipe: 27
Calories per serving: 290

V if using free-range eggs

4 egg whites
180 g (6 oz) caster sugar
1 tablespoon icing sugar, sifted
1 tablespoon unsweetened cocoa powder + extra, for dusting
a few drops of white wine vinegar
300 g (10 oz) low-fat fromage frais
2 × 420 g (14 oz) canned black cherries in juice, drained

❶ Preheat the oven to Gas Mark 4/180°C/350°F. Line a square baking tray with baking parchment.

❷ In a large bowl whisk the egg whites until very stiff, then continue to whisk, adding the caster sugar a spoonful at a time. Whisk well between each addition.

❸ Fold in the icing sugar, cocoa powder and vinegar. Pile the mixture on to the prepared baking tray and, using a spatula, level it.

❹ Bake for 15–20 minutes or until firm on the top and soft in the middle. Set aside for 5 minute to cool.

❺ Place a sheet of greaseproof paper on a worktop. Turn out the meringue on to the fresh sheet of greaseproof paper and carefully remove the baking parchment. Spread with the low-fat fromage frais, leaving a 2.5 cm (1-inch) border all around. Scatter over the black cherries. Roll up like a swiss roll, lifting the paper as you go. Place the roll on to a serving dish and, just before serving, dust with a little cocoa powder. Chill until required.

Cook's note: this meringue roulade will crack when rolled, but don't worry – it'll still look and taste wonderful. Simply stick it together with a little more filling as you roll. A last minute dusting with cocoa powder gives a stunning result.

This has to be the simplest table decoration of all. Take a pretty vase, glass plate or wire basket and fill with Christmas baubles. This is most effective if you use only two colours and one or two different sizes. Finish off with some curls of gold ribbon or feathers.

Instant Spiced Christmas Pudding

Serves: 10
Preparation time: 30 minutes + 2¹/₂ hours
  steaming
Freezing: not recommended
Points per serving: 3
Total Points per recipe: 30
Calories per serving: 220

Ⓥ if using free-range eggs

1 teaspoon sunflower oil
180 g (6 oz) dried apricots, chopped
120 g (4 oz) raisins
120 g (4 oz) sultanas
grated zest and juice of 2 large oranges
3 dessert apples, cored and grated
60 g (2 oz) molasses sugar
2 eggs
2 teaspoons ground cinnamon
1 teaspoon ground nutmeg
240 g (8 oz) brown breadcrumbs
2 tablespoons brandy (optional)

1 Grease a 1.2-litre (2-pint) pudding basin with the oil and line the base with greaseproof paper.
2 Place the apricots, raisins, sultanas, orange zest and juice in a large bowl. Add the remaining ingredients (except the brandy) and mix well. Spoon the mixture into the prepared pudding basin and level off the top. Cover the basin with a double thickness of aluminium foil and tie securely around the rim with string.
3 Steam the pudding for 2¹/₂ hours until the ingredients have fused together. Allow the cooked pud to stand for approximately 20 minutes before serving. Turn out and top with a little sprig of holly and, if you like, pour over the brandy and set it alight.

De-luxe Mince Parcels

Because these mince pies use filo pastry instead of shortcrust they contain less fat.

Makes: 12
Preparation and baking time: 30 minutes
Freezing: not recommended
Points per serving: 1¹/₂
Total Points per recipe: 18
Calories per serving: 110

Ⓥ

120 g (4 oz) vegetarian mincemeat
2 ripe bananas, diced finely
1 dessert apple, peeled, cored and chopped finely
6 large sheets filo pastry
1 egg, beaten
a pinch of salt
icing sugar, to dust

1 Preheat the oven to Gas Mark 6/200°C/400°F.
2 In a mixing bowl combine the mincemeat and fruit together. Set to one side.
3 Lay a sheet of filo pastry on the work surface. Brush with egg wash, top with a second sheet, brush again and top with a third sheet. Cut the layered filo pastry into 6 squares. Spoon a heap of the prepared mincemeat into the centre of each square and draw up the edges to form a ruffle. Repeat this process with the remaining sheets of filo.
4 Place the filo parcels on a non-stick baking tray and brush lightly with a little more egg wash. Bake for 6–7 minutes or until golden brown. Dust lightly with icing sugar. Serve warm.

Instant Spiced Christmas Pudding
De-luxe Mince Parcels

Instant Berry and Banana Ice-cream

This is a quick and totally easy way of making ice-cream. You can now buy a selection of exotic frozen fruits, which make a great alternative to raspberries. The secret of this instant ice-cream is to allow the fruit to thaw out only slightly.

Serves: 6
Preparation and cooking time: 5 minutes
Freezing: recommended
Points per serving: 1¹/₂
Total Points per recipe: 9
Calories per serving: 80

Ⓥ

480 g (1 lb) frozen red berries
180 g (6 oz) low-fat fromage frais
1 large ripe banana
1 teaspoon runny honey
2 tablespoons vodka (optional)
extra berries, for decoration
icing sugar, for dusting

❶ Place the frozen berries in a food processor and allow them to thaw out slightly (this should take about 10 minutes depending on how frozen they are and the temperature of your kitchen).

❷ Add the fromage frais, banana, honey and vodka, if using. Blend briefly or until combined and almost smooth – this should take about 30 seconds to 1 minute.

❸ Spoon the ice-cream into glasses. Garnish with the extra berries and dust with a little icing sugar. Serve at once or return to the freezer until needed.

Cook's note: if you are keeping this ice-cream in the freezer for any length of time, remember to remove it from the freezer at least 20–30 minutes before serving.

Pineapple Surprise

Serves: 6
Preparation time: 15 minutes
Freezing: not recommended
Points per serving: ¹/₂
Total Points per recipe: 3
Calories per serving: 50

Ⓥ

1 large, ripe pineapple

❶ Cut the top and bottom off the pineapple.
❷ Set the leafy top aside.
❸ With a small sharp knife, cut around the inside of the skin – do one end first and then the other.
❹ Carefully push through to release the pineapple from its skin.
❺ Stand the pineapple skin on a serving plate.

❻ Cut the tube of pineapple flesh into 1 cm (¹/₂-inch) slices and, using an apple corer, remove the centre from each slice.
❼ Pop the cored slices back into the pineapple skin.
❽ Replace the leafy top and serve with ginger syllabub.

Ginger Syllabub

Traditionally syllabub is a delectable rich cream, flavoured with sugar or honey and lemon. Here's a lighter version made with fromage frais.

Serves: 6
Preparation time: 15 minutes + steeping overnight
Freezing: not recommended
Points per serving: 1¹/₂
Total Points per recipe: 9
Calories per serving: 95

2 tablespoons sherry
a little freshly grated nutmeg
1 teaspoon ground ginger
a sprig of rosemary
2 teaspoons runny honey
grated zest and juice of 2 lemons
360 g (12 oz) low-fat fromage frais, chilled well
4 pieces of stem ginger, chopped finely
6 clementines
small sprigs of rosemary, to garnish (optional)

❶ Begin the night before you want to serve the dish. In a bowl combine the sherry, nutmeg, ground ginger, rosemary, honey, lemon zest and juice. Mix well and leave to stand overnight in the refrigerator.

❷ Next day, remove the rosemary from the infused liquid and discard. Fold the liquid into the chilled fromage frais with the chopped stemmed ginger.

❸ Segment the clementines and place in the bottom of 6 wine glasses. Spoon the ginger cream into the wine glasses and decorate each with a small sprig of rosemary and a sprinkling of grated nutmeg. Chill until required.

Here are some more ideas for quick and easy Christmas decorations. Simple stencils are widely available now from craft shops. Use them with special stencil wax crayons to create festive designs on paper napkins.
(See our table setting on page 39.)
For a pressie for a child (and here we're talking about children aged 3 to 70!) add an extra dimension.
After wrapping and tying, slip a tiny gift under the ribbon. For our table setting on page 45 we used coloured wax crayons, but anything bright and colourful and cheap would do.
Easy place-names: use super-glue to stick magnet letters (which you buy in toy shops) to stiff card to make names.
Decorate with gold stars or draw on squiggles with a gold pen. See page 47 for an example.

Odds and Ends

Here are some scrumptious recipes for leftovers. These are really imaginative ideas for the week between Christmas and New Year – from quick and delicious snacks through to lunches and suppers, and a not turkey curry in sight!

Turkey Pizza Pie

Serves: 6
Preparation and cooking time: 45 minutes
Freezing: not recommended
Points per serving: 4
Total Points per recipe: 24
Calories per serving: 230

240 g (8 oz) packet of pizza dough mix
2 courgettes, sliced lengthways
1 small aubergine, cut into 1 cm (^{1}/2-inch) slices
4 tablespoons fat-free french dressing
240 g (8 oz) tomato and herb pizza sauce
240 g (8 oz) cooked turkey or gammon, cut
    into strips
60 g (2 oz) parmesan cheese, grated
salt and freshly ground black pepper
a bunch of fresh basil, to serve (optional)

❶ Preheat the oven to Gas Mark 7/220°C/425°F.
❷ Make up the pizza dough following the instructions on the packet. Shape the dough into a round and on a lightly floured surface roll out to a 25 cm (12-inch) diameter. Lift the round on to a non-stick baking sheet.
❸ Preheat the grill. Brush the sides of the courgette and aubergine with the fat-free dressing and grill until golden, turning once. Spoon the tomato and

herb sauce over the pizza base. Scatter the turkey or gammon strips over the base and lay the grilled slices of courgette and aubergine on top. Season with freshly ground black pepper.
❹ Scatter the parmesan cheese on top and bake for 15–20 minutes or until bubbling hot and cooked. Scatter over the basil leaves (if using) and serve at once.

This is quick and simple for a special meal: cut Christmas trees or other festive shapes out of shiny green card.
Place by each plate and put the place-setting and rolled napkin on top.
For a snowman chain, take some brown paper and fold up like a concertina – make the folds about 5 cm (2 inches) apart and do it as exactly as you can. Now draw a snowman with a top hat on the top fold; the arms of the snowman should go off at the sides. Cut out and unfold your chain. Use a thick felt-tip or marker pens to colour in scarves and top hats.
Use a finer pen for faces and buttons. Hang up or use to decorate the table.

Savoury Bread Pudding

Serves: 6

Preparation and cooking time: 1 hour + standing overnight

Freezing: not recommended

Points per serving: $4^1/_2$

Total Points per recipe: 27

Calories per serving: 270

5 slices granary bread, cut in half

3 eggs

300 ml ($^1/_2$ pint) skimmed milk

120 g (4 oz) mature low-fat Cheddar, grated

2 tablespoons coarse-grained mustard

240 g (8 oz) cooked gammon, sliced thinly

480 g (1 lb) small ripe tomatoes, sliced thickly

$^1/_2$ bunch of spring onions, chopped

1 tablespoon chopped fresh thyme or 1 teaspoon dried

salt and freshly ground black pepper

❶ Arrange the bread on the bottom of an ovenproof dish, overlapping the slices slightly.

❷ In a food processor, blend the eggs, skimmed milk, Cheddar and mustard together. Season with pepper and set aside.

❸ Lay the gammon slices over the bread and top with a layer of tomatoes. Scatter over the spring onions and thyme and season well.

❹ Pour over the egg mixture, cover with clingfilm and place in the refrigerator for 2 hours or overnight, to allow the mixture to soak into the bread completely.

❺ Preheat the oven to Gas Mark 5/190°C/375°F.

❻ Bake the savory pudding for 40 minutes. It should be browned on top and a knife inserted into the middle should come out clean. Serve at once with a crisp green salad.

Turkey on Rye

This is something really special in the sandwich line, which makes a lovely quick lunch when friends come round.

Serves: 4

Preparation time: 10 minutes

Freezing: not recommended

Points per serving: 3

Total Points per recipe: 12

Calories per serving: 150

4 slices thick granary or rye bread

a handful of salad leaves

1 tablespoon low-Calorie mayonnaise

2 tablespoons low-fat fromage frais

1 tablespoon coarse-grained mustard

240 g (8 oz) sliced cooked turkey, cut in strips

180 g (6 oz) grapes de-seeded and halved

1 punnet of mustard and cress

salt and freshly ground black pepper

❶ Place each slice of bread on a plate and top with salad leaves.

❷ In a mixing bowl combine the mayonnaise, fromage frais and mustard, and season with salt and pepper. Gently fold in the turkey and grapes and pile the mixture on top of the bread. Scatter each open sandwich with mustard and cress and grind over some extra black pepper. Serve at once.

Rapid Risotto

Serves: 4
Preparation and cooking time: 40 minutes
Freezing: not recommended
Points per serving: 6
Total Points per recipe: 24
Calories per serving: 370

2 teaspoons sunflower oil
1 onion, chopped
2 celery sticks, chopped
2 large carrots, peeled and diced finely

2 teaspoons turmeric (optional)
2 garlic cloves, crushed
240 g (8 oz) easy-cook brown rice or risotto rice
1.2 litres (2 pints) vegetable stock
1 bay leaf
240 g (8 oz) frozen peas
240 g (8 oz) cooked turkey or gammon, sliced
    and cut into thin strips
2 tablespoons chopped fresh parsley
grated zest of 1 lemon
salt and freshly ground black pepper

❶ Heat the oil in a large saucepan and fry the onion, celery, and carrots for 4 minutes.
❷ Add the turmeric (if using), garlic and rice and cook for 30 seconds. Pour in the stock and stir in the bay leaf. Season well, cover and simmer for 20–25 minutes until the rice is tender. Add some extra liquid if the rice becomes dry.

❸ Add the peas and gammon or turkey. Leave the lid off the pan and cook for a further 5 minutes. Spoon the risotto into large soup bowls. Mix the parsley and lemon zest together and sprinkle over the risotto. Serve at once.

Gammon and Apple Toastie

Serves: 4
Preparation time: 10 minutes + 40–50 minutes
    cooking
Freezing: not recommended
Points per serving: 6¹/₂
Total Points per recipe: 26
Calories per serving: 360

8 slices of bread
240 g (8 oz) cooked gammon, sliced thinly
120 g (4 oz) half-fat Edam cheese, grated
2 dessert apples, cored and sliced thinly
2 tablespoons fat-free vinaigrette
salad leaves
freshly ground black pepper

❶ Preheat the grill and lightly toast the bread on both sides.
❷ Lay the slices of gammon over 4 slices of toast (keeping the remaining toast warm). Top with the grated Edam and return to the grill until the cheese just melts.
❸ Meanwhile in a frying-pan fry the apple slices in the vinaigrette until just beginning to soften.

❹ Remove the toasted gammon and cheese from the grill and put on 4 plates. Season with pepper. Spoon over the hot apple slices with any juices and top with the remaining slices of toast. Cut in half and surround with the salad leaves. Serve at once.

Index